by Tyler Feder

 Dial Books for Young Readers

For Coco and Spinny ♡

DIAL BOOKS FOR YOUNG READERS
An imprint of Penguin Random House LLC, New York

First published in the United States of America by Dial Books for Young Readers,
an imprint of Penguin Random House LLC, 2021

Visit us online at penguinrandomhouse.com.

Library of Congress Cataloging-in-Publication Data
Names: Feder, Tyler, author, illustrator. | Title: Bodies are cool / by Tyler Feder.
Description: New York : Dial Books for Young Readers, 2021. | Audience: Ages 3-5. | Audience: Grades K-1.
| Summary: Illustrations and easy-to-read, rhyming text celebrate bodies of all shapes, sizes, ages,
and colors, with different kinds of hair, eyes, spots, scars, and more. | Identifiers: LCCN 2020035586 (print) |
LCCN 2020035587 (ebook) | ISBN 9780593112625 (hardcover) | ISBN 9780593112632 (ebook) | ISBN 9780593112649 (ebook)
Subjects: CYAC: Stories in rhyme. | Human body—Fiction. | Classification: LCC PZ8.3.F3J3 Bod 2021 (print) | LCC PZ8.3.F3J3 (ebook)
| DDC [E]—dc23 | LC record available at https://lccn.loc.gov/2020035586
LC ebook record available at https://lccn.loc.gov/2020035587

Manufactured in China
10 9 8 7 6 5 4 3 2

Design by Jennifer Kelly | Text hand-lettered by Tyler Feder

The art for this book was drawn digitally, with love, by a left hand with a crooked index finger.

Big bodies, small bodies,
dancing, playing, happy bodies!

Look at all these different bodies!

Bodies are cool!

Lanky bodies, squat bodies,
tall, short, wide or narrow bodies,
somewhere-in-the middle bodies.
Bodies are cool!

Round bodies, muscled bodies,
curvy curves and straight bodies,
jiggly-wiggly fat bodies.
Bodies are cool!

Poofy hair, wavy hair, springy curls and flat hair, lots of hair or no hair. Bodies are cool!

Leg hair, armpit hair,
fuzzy-lip-and-chin hair,
brows-meet-in-the-middle hair.
Bodies are cool!

Hazel eyes, brown eyes,
monolids and round eyes,
blind and wearing-glasses eyes.
Bodies are cool!

Crooked faces, bump-nosed faces,
flat nose, full lips, gap-toothed faces,
stick-out ears and thin-lip faces.
Bodies are cool!

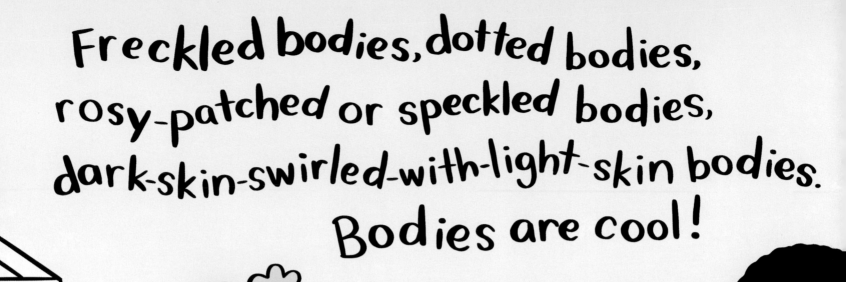

Freckled bodies, dotted bodies,
rosy-patched or speckled bodies,
dark-skin-swirled-with-light-skin bodies.
Bodies are cool!

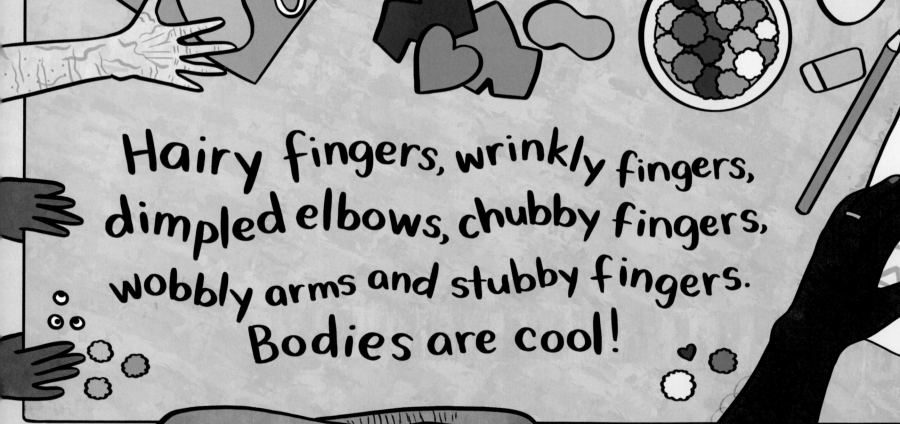

Hairy fingers, wrinkly fingers,
dimpled elbows, chubby fingers,
wobbly arms and stubby fingers.
Bodies are cool!

Soft tummies, saggy tummies,
flat or sticky-outy tummies,
innies, outies, pregnant tummies.
Bodies are cool!

Thick legs, scrawny legs,
knobby knees and long legs,
roll-up-to-the-table legs.
Bodies are cool!

Faint scars, bold scars,
stripes-from-getting-bigger scars,
marks-that-tell-a-story scars.
Bodies are cool!

Growing bodies, aging bodies,
features-rearranging bodies,

magic ever-changing bodies.
Bodies are cool!

My body, your body,
every different kind of body!
All of them are good bodies!

BODIES ARE COOL!